60

MAY 2003

0 03 03 0247453 8

+
599.7
m

W9-DDL-903

WITHDRAWN
MENASHA'S PUBLIC LIBRARY

Pandas

Patricia Kendell

RAINTREE STECK-VAUGHN PUBLISHERS
RSVP®

A Harcourt Company

Austin   New York
www.raintreesteckvaughn.com

Youth Department
Menasha's Public Library
440 1st Street
Menasha, WI 54952

in the wild

Alligators   Chimpanzees   Dolphins   Elephants
Gorillas   Grizzly Bears   Leopards   Lions
Pandas   Polar Bears   Sharks   Tigers

© Copyright 2002, text, Steck-Vaughn Company

All rights reserved. No part of this book may be reproduced or utilized in any form or by any means, electronic or mechanical, including photocopying, recording, or by any information storage and retrieval system, without permission in writing from the Publishers. Inquiries should be addressed to: Copyright Permissions, Steck-Vaughn Company, P.O. Box 26015, Austin, TX 78755.

Published by Raintree Steck-Vaughn Publishers, an imprint of Steck-Vaughn Company

Library of Congress Cataloging-in-Publication Data is available upon request

ISBN 0-7398-5500-X

Printed in Hong Kong. Bound in the United States.

1 2 3 4 5 6 7 8 9 0 LB 07 06 05 04 03 02

Photograph acknowledgments:
Heather Angel 1 & 18, 3 (first, second, & fourth), 4, 10, 11, 14, 15, 19, 21, 23, 24, 25, 29, 32;
Bruce Coleman Inc. cover & 12 (Orion Press), 5, 16, 17;
Corbis 6, 7, 8 (Karen Su);
FLPA 3 (third), 13 (Sunset), 20 (Mark Newman), 22 (Gerard Lacz), 28 (David Hosking);
Still Pictures 9 (Roland Seitre);
WWF-UK 26, 27 (Stuart Chapman).

All instructions, information, and advice given in this book are believed to be reliable and accurate. All guidelines and warnings should be read carefully, and the author, packager, editor, and publisher cannot accept responsibility for injuries or damage arising out of failure to comply with the same.

Contents

Where Giant Pandas Live

Giant pandas live in the cool mountain forests of western China.

They belong to the bear family and are among the most **endangered** animals in the world.

Baby Pandas

A mother panda usually has only one baby at a time. When it is born, the **cub** is tiny, helpless, and weighs only 5–7 ounces.

This cub was born in a **den** made in the hollow of a tree.

Looking After the Cub

The cub drinks milk from its mother until it is
1 year old. Mother pandas lick their cubs clean.

This panda is cuddling her cub to keep it warm.

Keeping Safe

Panda cubs are in danger from many different animals. The leopard is one of their enemies.

Cubs soon learn how to climb trees—away from danger. Although adult pandas are big animals, they are expert climbers.

Family Life

A mother and cub make up a panda family.
They stay close together in their **territory**.

Cubs begin to eat bamboo leaves when they are about 8 months old. Their mothers teach them where to find the best kind of bamboo.

Leaving Home

A panda cub stays with its mother until it is 2 to 3 years old. Then it has to find its own territory.

Male pandas roam over a wide area.
They will fight with other males to win a **mate**.

Eating

Pandas eat mainly bamboo. This panda is holding the bamboo and nibbling the juiciest parts.

When bamboo has grown flowers and turned
to seed, it dies. This panda will now have
to travel long distances to find new bamboo.

Drinking

This panda has eaten a lot of juicy bamboo,
but it is still thirsty.

Pandas need to drink about twice a day.
They sometimes drink river water and
have been seen licking snow.

Rest and Play

Pandas spend up to 14 hours every day searching for bamboo. After a good meal, the panda rests.

Pandas sometimes roll in the snow. They do this for
fun and to clean their fur.

21

Keeping in Touch

Pandas mainly live alone, but they do keep in touch with one another. Their low growls travel through the forest to other pandas.

They also leave **scent marks** and scratches on trees, so other pandas know where they are.

Pandas in Danger

Pandas are in great danger because much
of their forest home has been cut down
to make more space for people to live.

Towns and roads now divide up the forest. This makes it more difficult for the shy panda to move through the forest in search of bamboo.

More Dangers

There are laws to protect pandas. However, people still kill them for their valuable fur.

Some pandas are accidentally killed in traps set for other animals. These men will make sure that no more pandas are caught in this trap.

Helping Pandas to Survive

Some people hoped that if pandas were safe in a zoo, they would have more babies. Sadly, this has not happened.

The best hope for pandas is to protect the forest homes where they are free to roam and have enough to eat.

Further Information

ORGANIZATIONS TO CONTACT

World Wildlife Fund
1250 24th Street, N.W.
Washington, D.C. 20037
(202) 293-4800
www.worldwildlife.org/fun/kids.cfm

American Museum of Natural History
Central Park West at 79th Street
New York, NY 10024-5199
212 769-5000
www.amnh.org

BOOKS

Fowler, Allan. *Giant Pandas: Gifts from China*. Danbury, CT: Children's Press, 1995.

Freeman, Marcia S. *Giant Pandas*. Dover, NH: Pebble Books, 1999.

Granfield, Linda. *The Legend of the Panda*. Plattsburgh, NY: Tundra Books, 2001.

Traqui, Valerie. *The Panda: Wild About Bamboo*. Watertown, MA: Charlesbridge Publishing, 1999.

Glossary

WEBSITES

Most young children will need adult help when visiting websites. Those listed have child-friendly pages to bookmark.

www.panda.org/kids/wildlife
WWF's virtual wildlife site has information about why the panda is endangered and what is being done to save it.

http://animal.discovery.com
This site includes a virtual journey to China called "Meet the Pandas."

http://pandas.si.edu/kids
The Smithsonian site has a range of activities for young children including a quiz, crosswords, and a "Saving Great Pandas" activity book to download.

http://www.thebigzoo.com/Animals/Giant_Panda.asp
This site has information about pandas with photographs and details of children's books.

cub – (KUB) a young animal, in this case, a young panda.

den – (DEN) a wild animal's home.

endangered – (en-DAYN-jurd) when there is a danger that all the animals of one kind, such as pandas, could die or be killed.

mate – (MATE) to make babies.

scent marks – (SENT MARKS) when pandas leave a special smell on a tree.

territory – (TER-uh-tor-ee) the home area of an animal.

Index

© 2002 White-Thomson Publishing Ltd